Roomemory

The Greek Lyrical Poet Simonidies of Ceos is commonly credited with developing the most potent of memory aides the Method of Loci. After a banquet the roof of the banquet hall collapsed leaving Simonidies as the only one to escape. When asked to remember the guests who had been present he found that by visualising their position in the hall he was able to remember each diner and their specific position.

Given the fantastic ability of children to both learn and incorporate new techniques into their developing brain I designed this Colouring book to help parents to introduce the technique as early as possible. I have also designed a challenge to prove to you the power of the Method of Loci.

Challenge:

1. Read the following list of animals aloud to both yourself and your children:

Ant, Baboon, Cat, Duck, Fish, Goat, Hawk, Insect, Jackal, Kangaroo, Lion, Moose, Newt, Owl, Parrot, Quail, Ram, Snake, Toad, Urchin, Vulture, Weasel, Yak and Zebu.

2. Take turns trying to remember as many of the animals as you can in the same order you find them above.

3. After colouring the animals into each and every room of your imaginary house, cut out the animals found on the last three pages and have your children place them around your real home, taking care to place them in the same place you find them in the colouring book illustrations.

4. Now try to remember the list of animals again while imagining yourself walking through the house placing the cut outs.

I think you will find that you're on your way to becoming a truly superior memoriser.

Copyright © 2013 Jason Leonard. All rights reserved.
First paperback edition in Canada 2013
A catalogue record for this book is available from Library and Archives Canada.
ISBN978-0-993633-40-9
No part of this book shall be reproduced or transmitted in any form or by any means electronic or mechanical, including photocopying, recording, or by any information retrieval system without written permission of the publisher.
Published by JR Press.
Designed and Set by JR Press
Printed in Great Britain

Upon My pillow sits

An ant wearing pants

Beside my Bed

A Baboon licking a spoon

Upon the window sill

A Cat wearing a hat

Beside the Desk

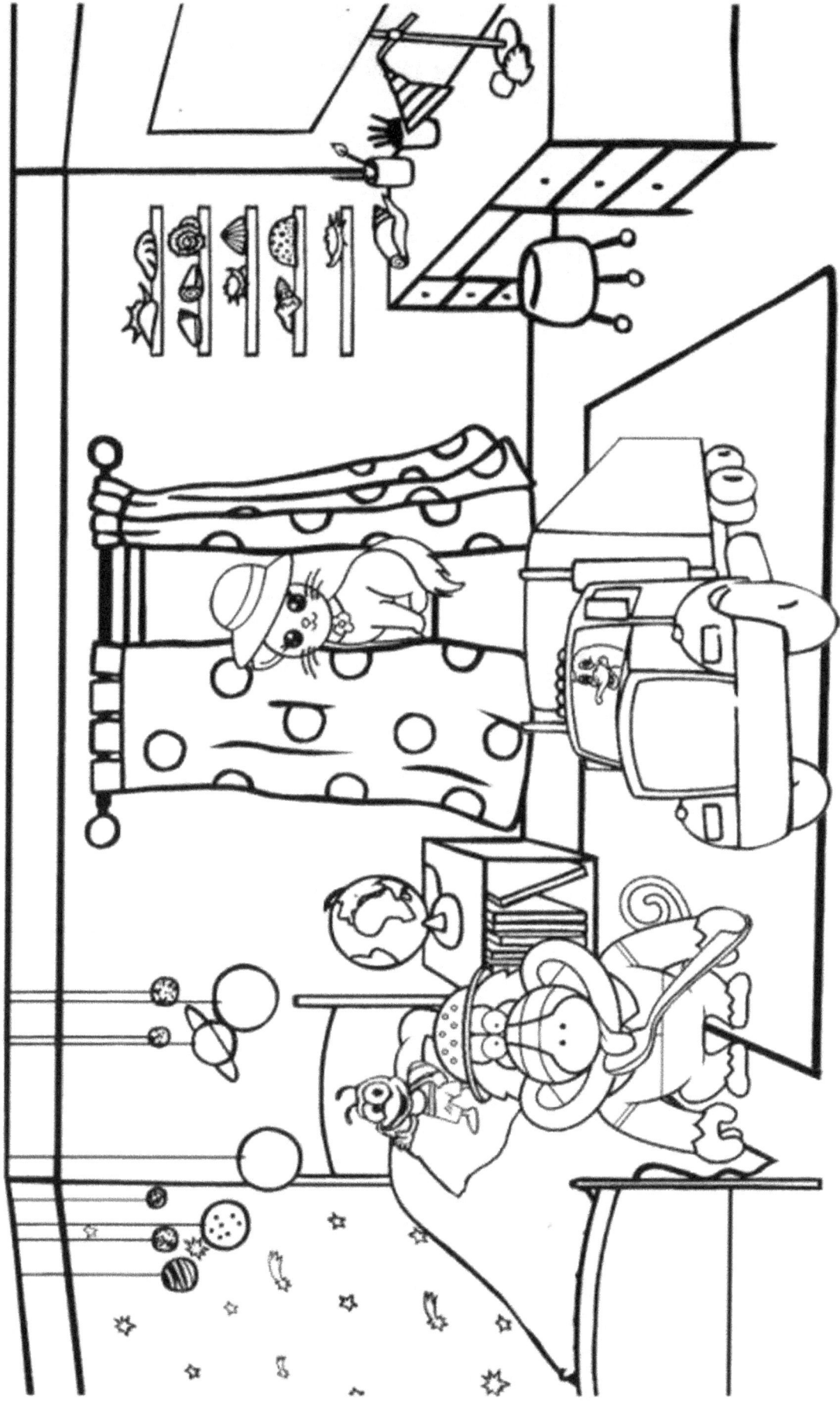

A Duck driving a Truck

Out the Door

A Fish in a Dish

In the Hall

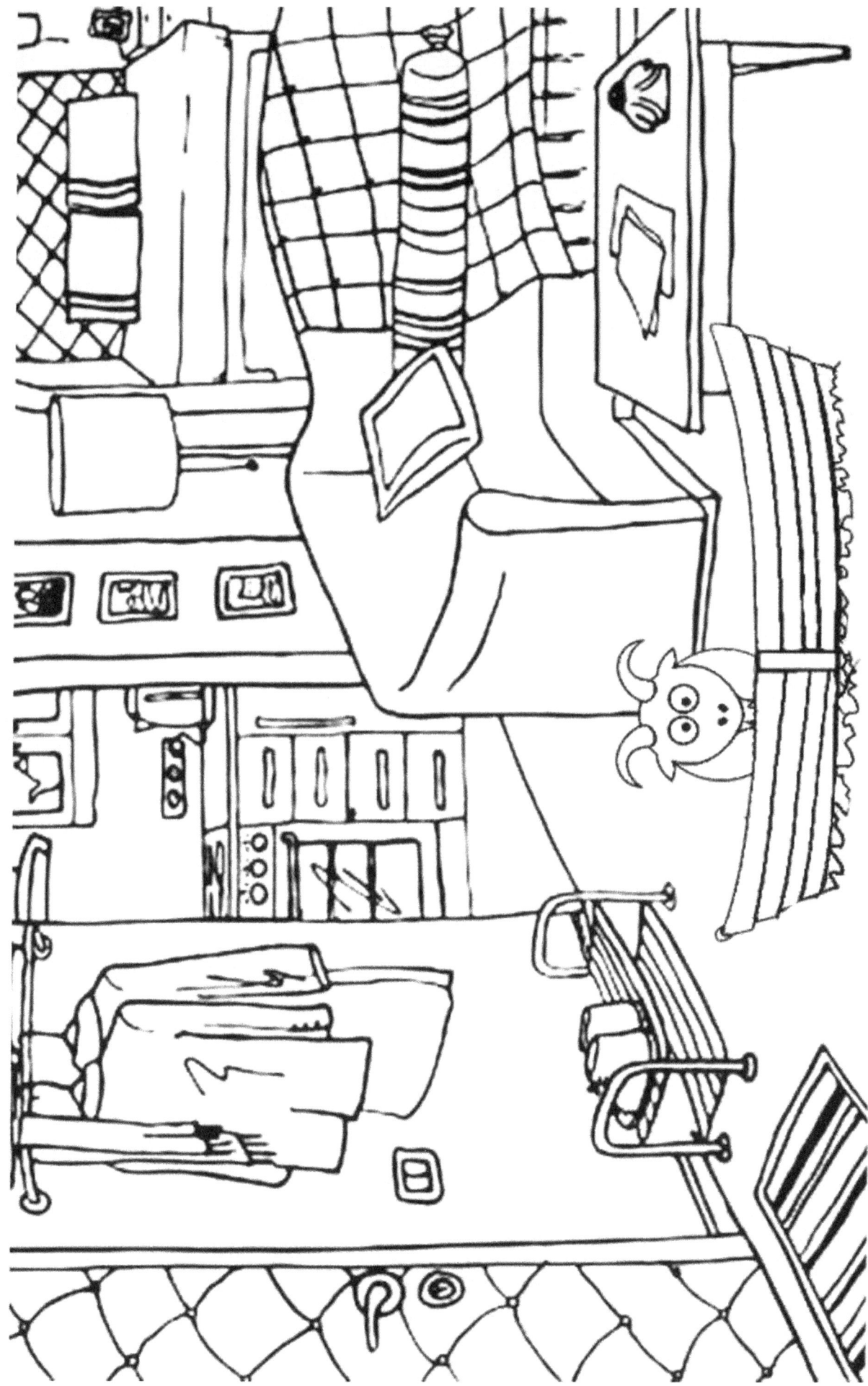

A Goat in a Boat

Past the Bathroom Door

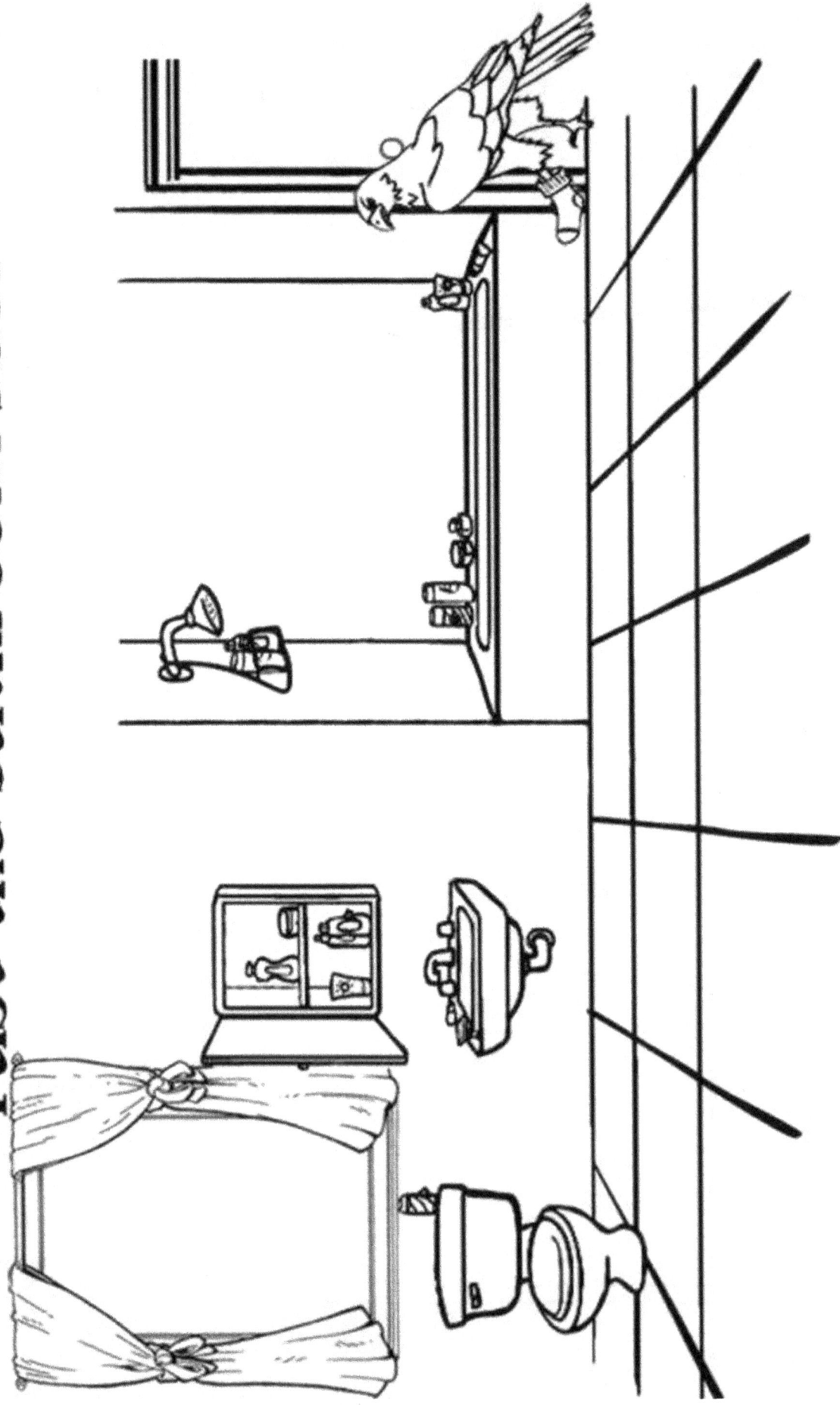

A Hawk wearing a Sock

In the Bathtub

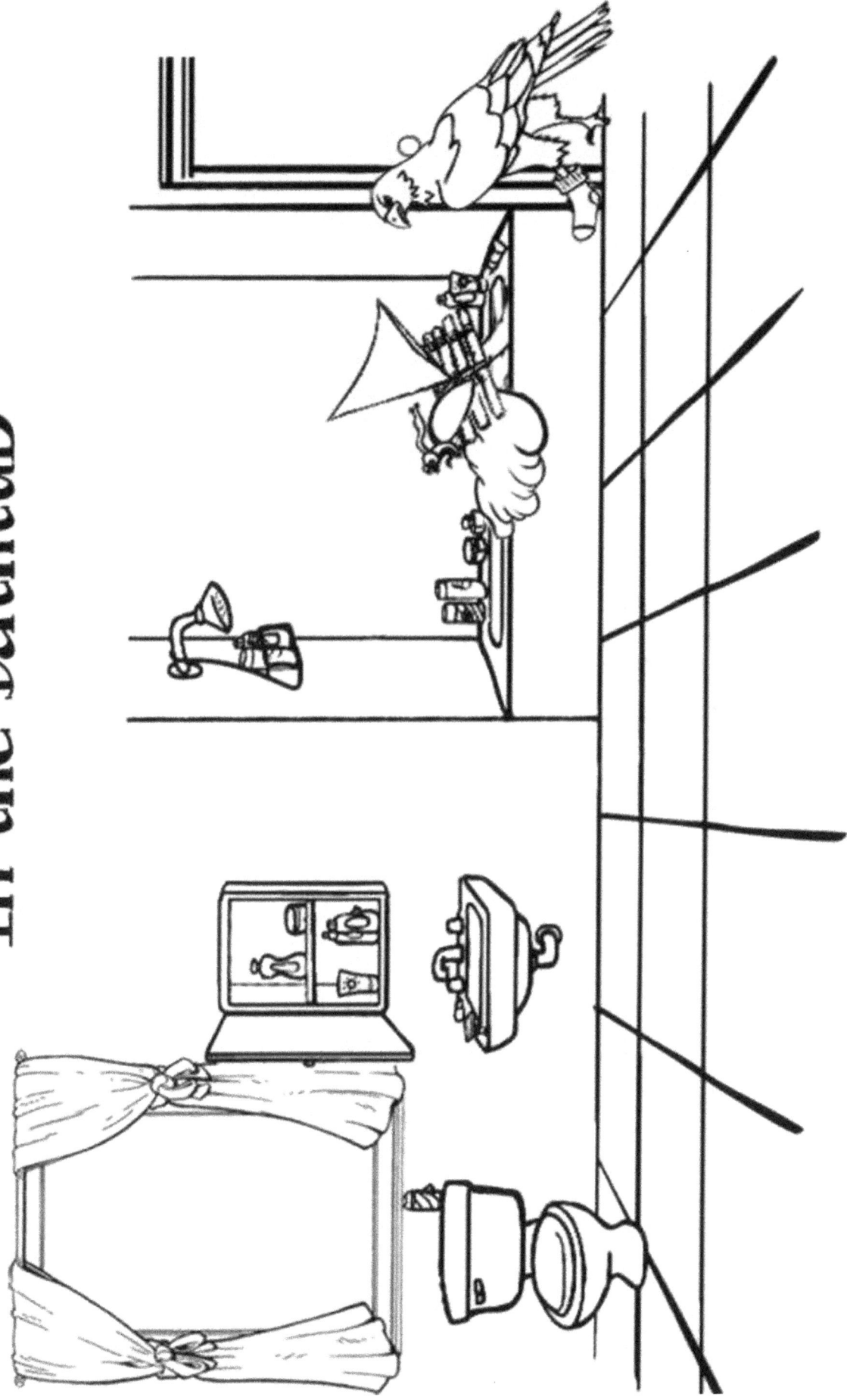

An insect that's been shipwrecked

In the Sink

A Jackal in a shackle

Upon the Tap

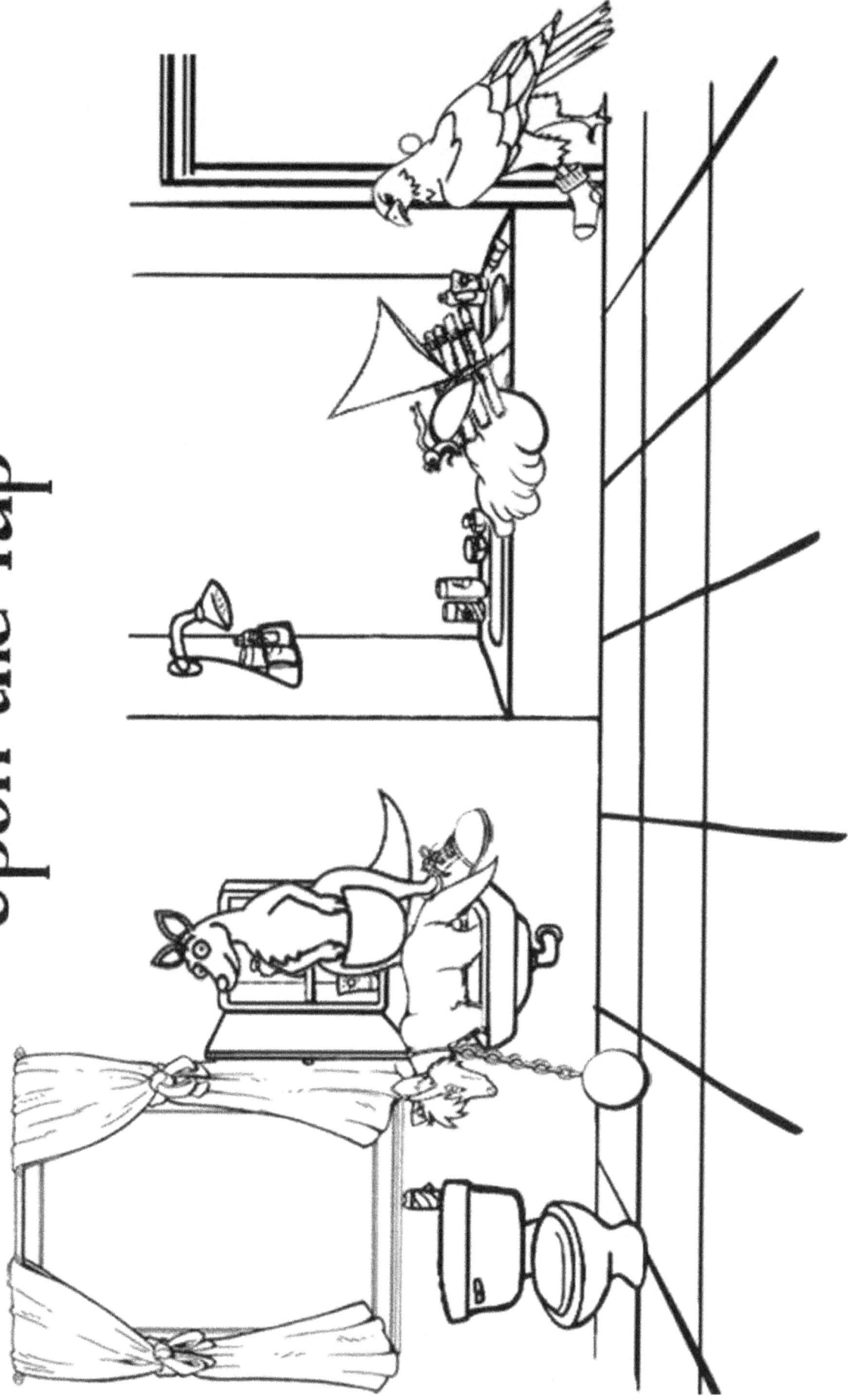

A kangaroo with a shoe

In the window

A Lion who is crying

Upon the Toilet

A Moose drinking Juice

In the Kitchen

A Newt eating fruit

In the In In the Fridge

An Owl in a towel

In the Cupboard

A parrot and his carrot

On the Stove

A quail in a pail

In the Sink

A Ram eating Jam

On the Tap

A Snake eating cake

Perched upon the Dishwasher

A Toad who somehow glowed

Out the Front Door

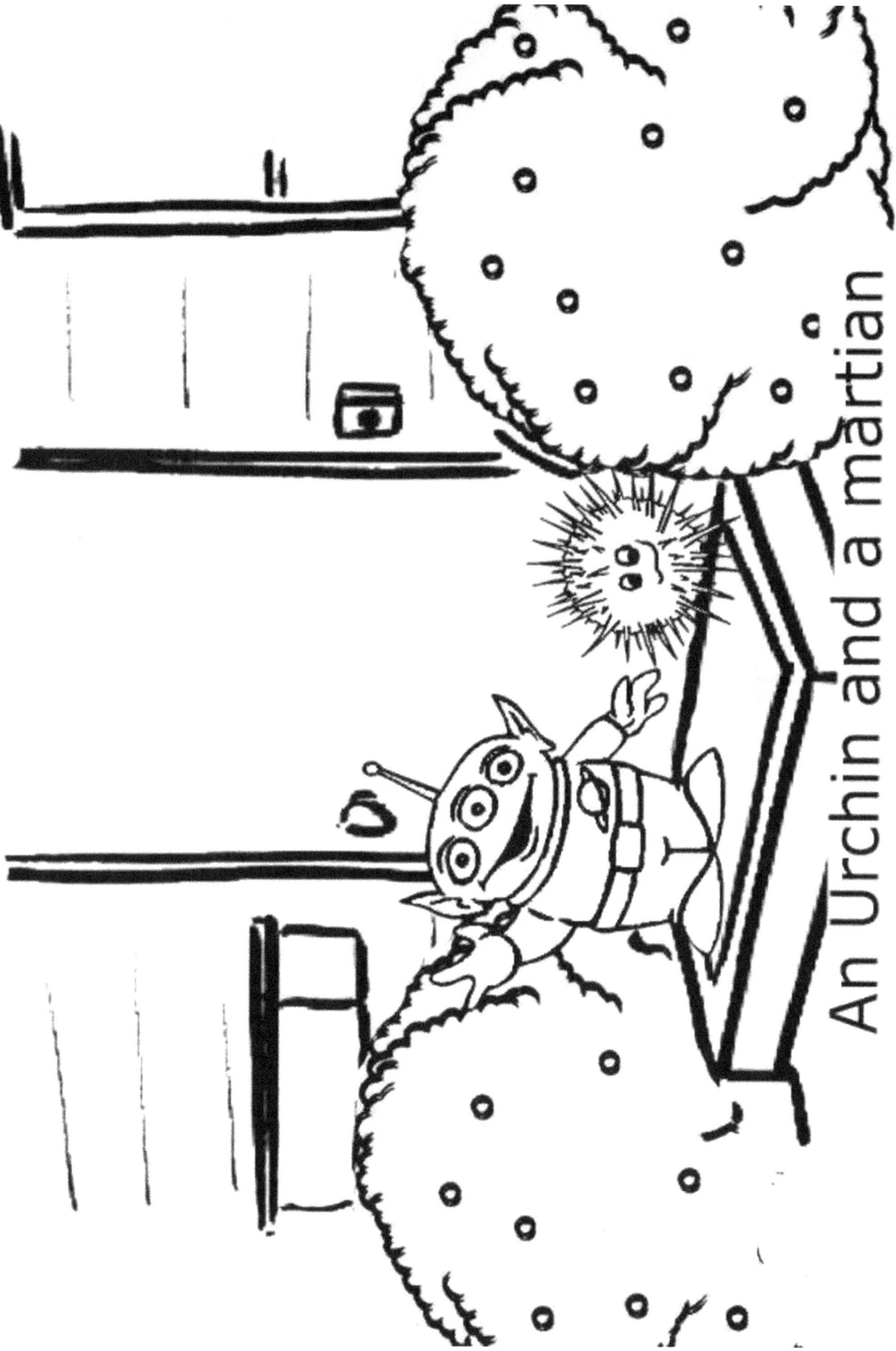

An Urchin and a martian

On the Grass

a Vulture carves a sculpture

In the Shed

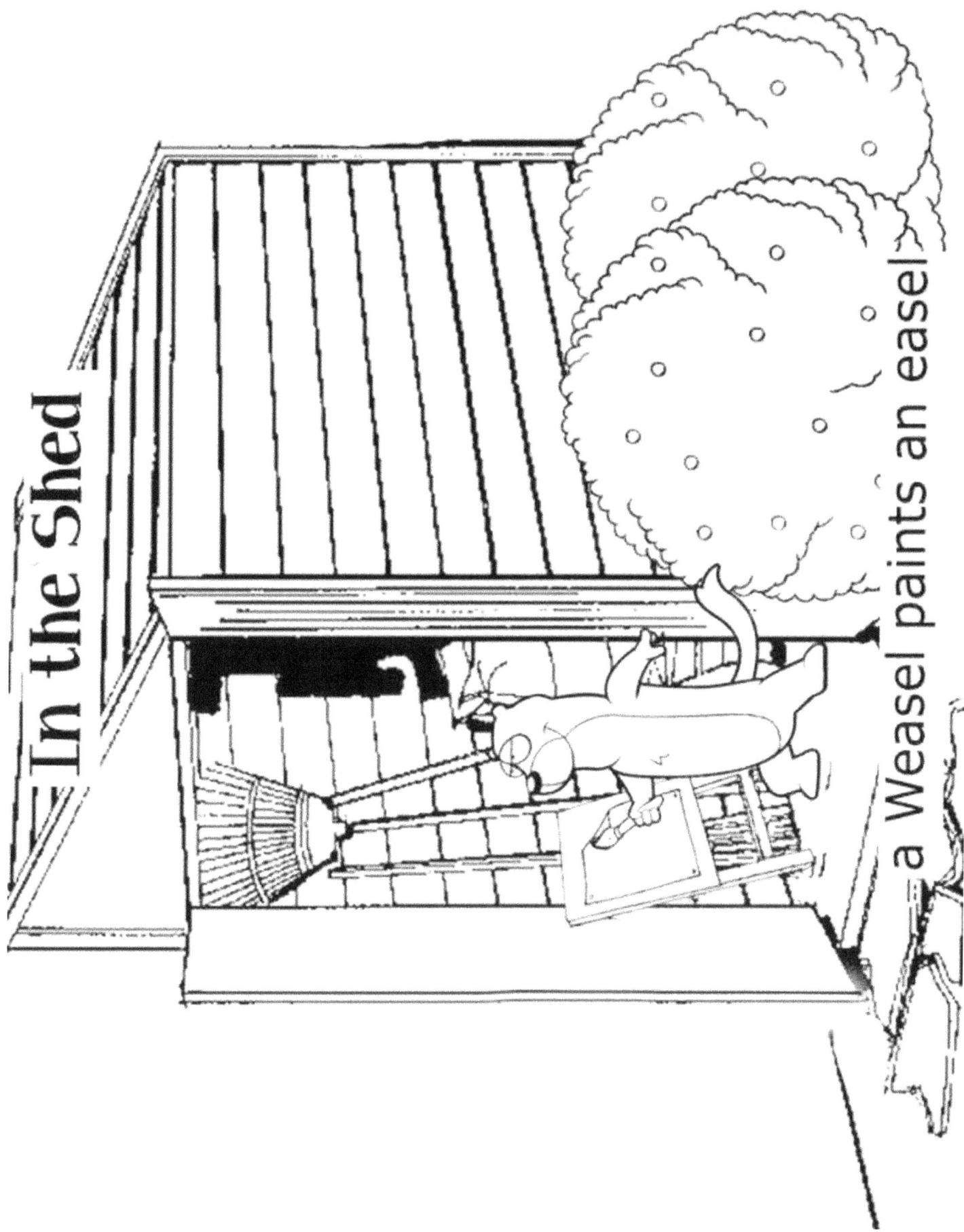

a Weasel paints an easel

On the Driveway

A Yak holding a sack

On the Road

a Zebu in a lean-to